THE ORIGINAL OLYMPICS

Stewart Ross

WAYLAND

ANCIENT GREECE

Daily Life
Gods and Goddesses
Greek Theatre
The Original Olympics

Front cover: A vase painting of a Greek horse race, from about 490 BC. Stirrups had not been invented, so there was more of a chance that riders would fall off when they galloped.

Series editors: Katrina Maitland Smith and Jill A. Laidlaw
Book editor: Jill A. Laidlaw
Design: Stonecastle Graphics Ltd
Consultant: Dr Angus M. Bowie, Lobel Fellow in Classics at the Queen's College, University of Oxford

This edition published in 1999 by Wayland Publishers Ltd
First published in 1996 by Wayland (Publishers) Ltd,
61 Western Road, Hove, East Sussex, BN3 1JD

The quotations in this book have been translated and, in some cases, adapted from their translations, to make them easier to read.

British Library Cataloguing in Publication Data
Ross, Stewart
   Original Olympics. - (Ancient Greece Series; Vol. 1)
   I. Title II. Series
   796.480938

ISBN 0 7502 2556 4

Photographic acknowledgements
The publishers would like to thank the following sources for providing the photographs for this book: **AKG, London** 17; **All Sport** 42, 43 (all, IOC), 44 (Bob Martin), 45 (top, Simon Bruty); **Ancient Art & Architecture/Ronald Sheridan** 9, 15, 23, 26-7, 29, 36, 39, 44 (bottom); **Bridgeman Art Library** 5, 25, 33; **C.M. Dixon** 6 (top), 8, 10, 11, 14, 30; **Robert Harding Picture Library** 6-7 (bottom); **Michael Holford** cover, 18, 19, 20-21, 24, 26 (inset), 28-9, 31, 32, 34, 35, 37, 38, 40, 41.
Illustration and map design: HardLines

Typesetting and reproduction by Pageturn Ltd
Printed and bound by Eurografica, Italy

CONTENTS

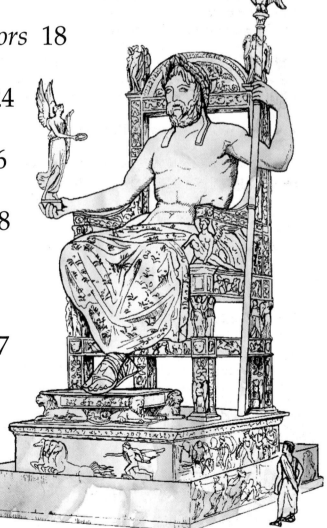

1 The Great Sacrifice

Most of the crowd had stayed at the Olympic site overnight. At first light they began to stir. Rubbing the sleep from their eyes, they crawled out of their tents or unwrapped themselves from their blankets. They wandered down to the River Alpheios to wash, then looked around for breakfast. Some people had brought their food with them, others bought fresh bread and honey from the stall keepers who had travelled from the nearby village of Pisa during the night.

A great Games

As they ate, the spectators chatted among themselves. So far, they agreed, it had been a great Olympics. This year's programme had started with the boys' games and opening celebrations. The second day had seen exciting competitions, with chariot and horse races in the morning, and a pentathlon in the afternoon.

By half past eight in the morning the sun was already hot. Athletes were exercising in the gymnasium, loosening their limbs and practising their starts. A huge crowd, at least 50,000 strong, was gathering in front of the Temple of Zeus, ready for the great procession and sacrifice.

This is a bronze statue of Zeus, the king of the Greek gods. Zeus was supposed to live on Mount Olympus, the highest mountain in Greece. The statue was made in the fifth century BC.

'The Olympic Games are pretty uncomfortable. You are scorched by the sun and crushed by the crowd. There are no decent toilets. You get soaked when it rains and you are deafened by the constant noise. But it's all worth it for the brilliant events you see.'

Epictetus, *Discourses*, c. AD 100.

ΑΒΓΔΕΖΗΘΙΚΛΜΝΞΟΠΡΣΤΥΦΧΨΩ

ΤΥΦΧΨ

Zeus, King of the Gods

The third-day procession and sacrifice was a tradition of every Olympic Games. It was a reminder of what the Games were really about – the greater glory of Zeus, King of the Gods.

The third day was chosen for the Olympic procession and sacrifice because it was right in the middle of the Games. The Games were always held during the summer and were arranged so that a full moon lit the celebrations on the third night.

The procession

When everything was ready, a trumpet blared and the procession moved off. It travelled all the way around the Altis, the sacred olive grove at Olympia (the name of the Olympic site).

First came the judges, then the ambassadors from the Greek city-states that had sent athletes to the Games. They were followed by the athletes. Finally, at the rear, tramping along in a huge cloud of dust, came the hundred oxen that were to be sacrificed on the Great Altar of Zeus.

The Great Altar of Zeus

The procession halted to the right of Zeus' Temple before the Great Altar. It was an amazing sight – the huge stone altar was covered with a pile of ashes 7 metres high. The ashes were left over from previous sacrifices of oxen. As the officials and athletes stood back, the oxen were driven forward.

Priests and officials made speeches. They dedicated the Games to Zeus and hoped that he would be pleased with the sacrifice he was about to receive.

A stone carving from the Parthenon temple in Athens. It shows an ox being led to sacrifice.

Sacrifice

When all was ready, slaves drove the oxen forward to the Altar and killed them one by one. The grass became slippery with blood. The bodies of the dead beasts were then butchered. Their thigh-bones were carried up the steps to the top of the altar and burned. The remainder of the carcasses were carried off to provide meat for the public feasts that evening.

> 'The statue of Zeus strikes terror into the hearts of all who see it. It is the custom of the athletes, as well as their fathers, brothers and trainers, to swear an oath beside the statue. With their hands on slices of boar's meat, they promise to obey the rules of the Olympic Games.'
>
> Pausanias, *Description of Greece*, c. AD 150.
> Pausanias was a Greek geographer and historian.

ΡΣΤΥΦΧΨ

ΔΕΖΗΘΙΚΛΜΝΞΟΠΡΣΤΥΦΧΨΩ

On with the Games

Before the slaughter was over, the crowd began to leave. The athletes returned to the gymnasium and their last-minute preparations. It would not be long now. After months of preparation, the eagerly awaited foot races were about to begin.

The gods take part in a procession. Zeus is third from the right, between his daughter Artemis (second from the right) and Athena, who gave her name to Athens.

2 Distant Beginnings

The ancient Greeks believed that the first Olympic Games were held in 776 BC. The first winner was Korebos, a young man from the city of Elis, the capital of the state in which the Games were held. He won a sprint race of about 200 metres.

Modern historians think that the Games began long before the time of Korebos, although they are not sure exactly when. Organized athletic sports probably began in Asia Minor (see map on page 22) during the tenth century BC. Some time after this, organized athletics caught on in Greece. Scholars believe that the first athletic contests were 'funeral games' that celebrated heroes killed in battle.

Several Greek legends tell us different versions of how the Games began.

A portrait of Heracles, on a gold coin from the rule of King Philip II, King of Macedon from 359 to 336 BC.

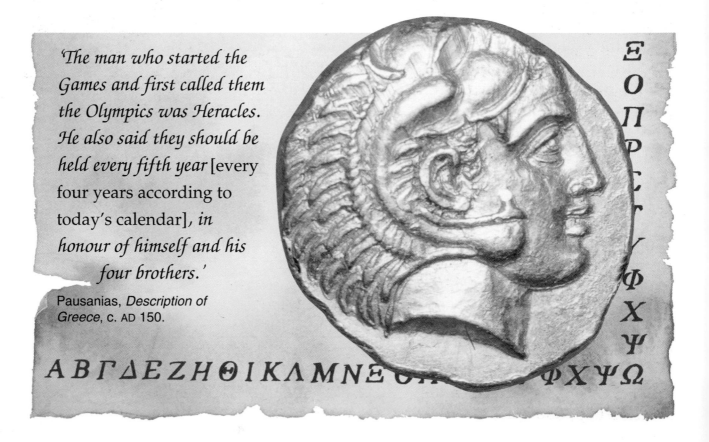

'The man who started the Games and first called them the Olympics was Heracles. He also said they should be held every fifth year [every four years according to today's calendar], in honour of himself and his four brothers.'

Pausanias, *Description of Greece*, c. AD 150.

ΑΒΓΔΕΖΗΘΙΚΛΜΝ

ΞΟΠΡΣΤΥΦΧΨΩ

Heracles

According to legends and poetry, the Greek hero Heracles was responsible for the foundation of the Games. One of the hero's twelve tasks (called the Labours of Heracles) was to clean out the massive stables of King Augeas of Elis. Heracles diverted the River Alpheios so that it flowed through the stables. When his task was over, Heracles celebrated by making a clearing in the sacred grove at Olympia and setting up the Games there to honour Zeus, his father.

This sculpture, from the Temple of Zeus at Olympia, shows Heracles holding up the world. This was another of his twelve Labours. The goddess Athena is helping him.

Pelops

Another story tells how Pelops wanted to marry Hippodamia, daughter of King Oenomaus of Elis. Oenomaus had been told he would be killed by his son-in-law, so he challenged everyone wishing to marry his daughter to a chariot race. If they won, they could marry Hippodamia. If they lost, they were killed. Because the king's chariot was pulled by horses that rode on the wind, he never lost.

Pelops bribed Oenomaus' charioteer to sabotage the king's chariot. A wheel spun off during the race and Oenomaus was killed. Legend says that Pelops then married Hippodamia and began the Olympic Games.

Zeus and Kronos

One story describes how Zeus and his father Kronos, the mightiest of the gods, came to fight. They battled on the mountains above the Altis to see which of them should own the world. Zeus won and became king of the gods. According to legend, Olympia's religious celebrations and Games were in honour of Zeus' triumph.

The ruins of the theatre and temple of Apollo at Delphi, where the famous oracle took place.

King Iphitos

King Iphitos of Elis lived around the ninth century BC. Legend says that he was upset that Greece was being destroyed by civil war and plague, so he went to ask the oracle at Delphi what he could do to set things right.

The oracle suggested that he should hold the Olympic Games and insist on a truce while they were going on. If there is any truth in this legend, then the Games were held during the time of Iphitos. This was well before Korebos' victory.

'When Iphitos restarted the Games, the people had forgotten the ancient customs. But as they remembered them, so new events were added to the Games.'

Pausanias, *Description of Greece*, c. AD 150.

ΑΒΓΔΕΖΗΘΙΚΛΜΝΞΟΠΡΣΤΥΦΧΨΩ

Υ Φ Χ Ψ

Other Games

Besides the Olympics, there were three other major Greek games:

- Isthmian Games. Held at Corinth in honour of Poseidon, the god of earthquakes and the sea.
- Pythian Games. Held at Delphi in honour of Apollo, a son of Zeus. Apollo was also the god of prophecy (telling the future), song and music.
- Nemean Games. Held at Nemea in honour of Zeus, like the Olympics.

The four major games made up a circuit of games at which all Greek men were welcome. The Olympics were the oldest games. There were minor games all over Greece. Whatever its size, each games was in honour of a god or a hero. The Greeks believed that only the gods could give them the strength needed for sporting victory.

The god Apollo, painted on the plate below, was admired for his beauty.

3 Olympia

As far as we know, the first athletic contests, which grew into the Olympics, were held at Olympia on the west coast of the Peloponnese. Olympia was originally a field planted with trees. The Hill of Kronos, named after Zeus' father, was next to the field. The Altis was at the foot of this hill. The River Kladeos ran down from the high mountains alongside the site.

By the sixth century BC temples, sports facilities and monuments had been built. Buildings were always being modified or pulled down and new ones put in their place. In this book the site is described as it may have looked in about 100 BC.

> '*There is no festival more glorious than Olympia!*'
>
> Pindar (c. 518-c. 438 BC), *Olympian Odes*. Pindar was a Greek poet famous for the works he wrote in honour of sporting champions.
>
> Τ Υ Φ Χ Ψ
> Ο Π Ρ Σ Τ Υ Φ Χ Ψ Ω

The stadium

For several hundred years, running races were held on a straight, level stretch of ground inside the Altis. The finish was near the Altar of Zeus. Spectators watched from the Hill of Kronos.

In about 350 BC, a new stadium was built outside the Altis. The track was about 192 metres long and about 35 metres wide. Legend said that Heracles fixed the length of the track by measuring out 600 of his own footsteps!

Earth was piled up round the track for 20,000 spectators to stand or sit on. So that everyone had a good view, the banks along the two longer sides curved in at the ends. A channel of water ran round the edge of the track. This gave spectators and runners a chance to refresh themselves during their long, hot day in the sun.

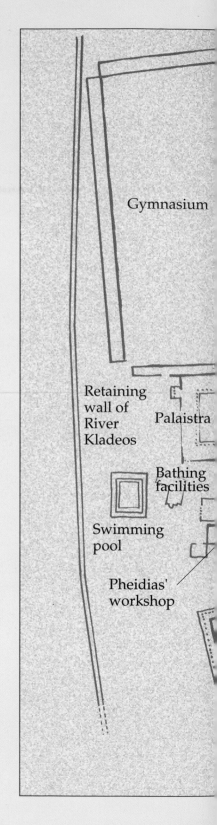

Gymnasium

Retaining wall of River Kladeos

Palaistra

Bathing facilities

Swimming pool

Pheidias' workshop

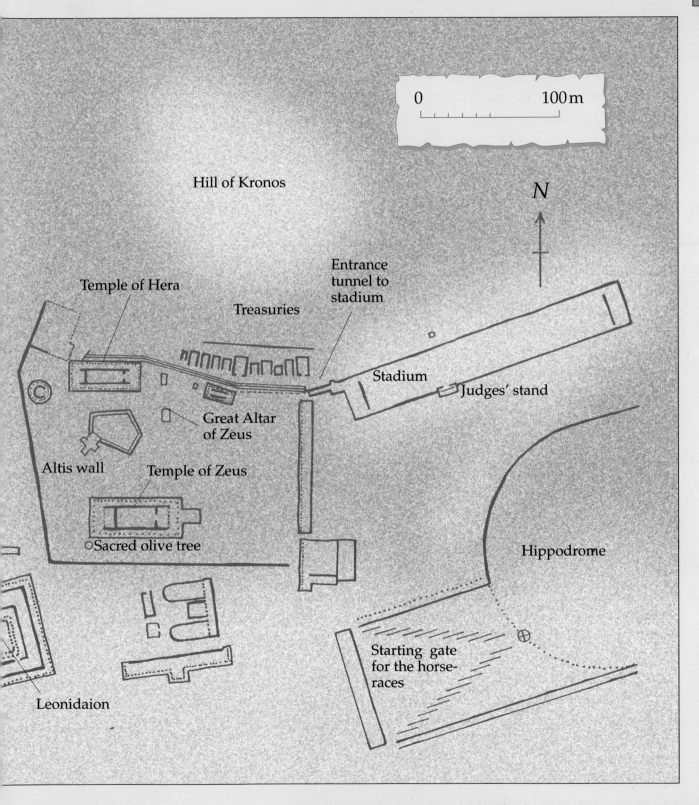

Hill of Kronos

0   100 m

N

Temple of Hera

Treasuries

Entrance
tunnel to
stadium

Stadium

Judges' stand

Great Altar
of Zeus

Altis wall

Temple of Zeus

Sacred olive tree

Hippodrome

Leonidaion

Starting gate
for the horse-
races

The hippodrome

Opposite the stadium was the *hippodrome*. Hippodrome means 'horse track' in Greek and it was here that the horse and chariot races took place. Unfortunately, most of the original hippodrome was washed away in floods, so it is difficult for us to understand how it was constructed.

As far as we can tell, there was a huge rectangular track, about 600 metres long and 200 metres wide. Competitors raced around pillars set in the middle of the track at each end. The pillar at the eastern end of the track had a statue of Pelops and Hippodamia on it. Races started from a complicated 'trap', similar to the stalls used in some horse races today. The starting gate led on to the western end of the track.

Athletes' facilities

As well as the stadium and hippodrome, there were several other buildings for the athletes' use. The most important ones were the baths, swimming pool, *palaistra* and gymnasium.

The Greeks were very keen on bathing after exercise. The bath house had

This athlete is holding a *strigil*, used for scraping oil off the body. The young slave boy is bringing him a towel and oil.

steam rooms (like a modern sauna) and hot and cold pools. Some rooms were warmed by under-floor heating, known as a *hypocaust*. The swimming pool was just for recreation, there were no swimming races in the ancient Olympic Games.

The palaistra was a large square building with a courtyard in the middle. The courtyard was used for training in fighting and jumping events. Along the sides, behind the rows of columns that held up the building, were nineteen rooms. These were practise rooms, common rooms, wash rooms and rooms for putting oil and powder on the athletes' bodies.

The gymnasium was like the palaistra in design, but much larger. Covered race tracks, the same length as that in the stadium, ran down the eastern side of the gymnasium. The space in the middle was used for throwing the discus and javelin.

'When we got to the gymnasium, we took off our clothes. One of us began to practise arm locks, while another tried neck holds.'

Lucian, *Lexiphanes*, c. AD 150.

ΡΣΤΥΦΧΨ
ΠΡΣΤΥΦΧΨΩ

Today, all that remains of the palaistra are rows of columns.

The Temple of Zeus

By the first century BC, a wall had been built around the Altis. Inside the wall were the Altar of Zeus, Pelops' burial mound, the Temple of Hera (Hera was the sister and wife of Zeus) and various other altars and monuments. The Temple of Zeus was the most magnificent by far. It took ten years to build and was finished in the middle of the fifth century BC.

The temple was a huge building resting on thirty-four columns. Inside stood one of the Seven Wonders of the Ancient World – a huge statue of Zeus by the famous Greek sculptor Pheidias. The seated figure was made out of wood, gold and ivory and was 13 metres high. Its head was adorned with a crown made of gold olive leaves. The statue's right hand held a figure of Nike, the winged goddess of victory. In the statue's left hand was a sceptre. It must have been a breathtaking sight.

Buildings and banks

All over the Olympic site there were other buildings, statues, altars and monuments. Beside the Temple of Zeus were the sacred olive tree and a second statue of Nike on a pillar 9 metres high. There was a large temple to Zeus' mother, the goddess Meter. Nearby was a monument to King Philip of Macedon, the father of Alexander the Great. Other buildings included a banqueting hall, a priests' house and a house for important visitors to stay in.

At the foot of the Hill of Kronos there was a row of eleven small 'treasuries'. These were set up by the people of Greek settlements overseas who wanted to be well thought of at Olympia. The treasuries were filled with money and precious objects. As a result, they were used as banks.

This statue of Nike was made in Greece around 150 BC.

'The image of Zeus was made by Pheidias. We know this because there is an inscription round the bottom of the statue: "The Athenian named Pheidias, son of Charmides, made me."'

Pausanias, *Description of Greece*, c. AD 150.

Σ
Τ
Υ
Φ
Χ
Ψ

ΜΝΞ ΟΠΡΣΤΥΦΧΨΩ

Historians think that Pheidias' statue of Zeus would have looked something like this (left).

17

4 Trainers, Judges and Spectators

The Olympic Games were so important to the Greeks that they dated events by them. Beginning with the Games of 776 BC, the Olympics took place every four years. This four year cycle was called an Olympiad. For example, Olympiad 2-1 was the name of the first year in the four-year cycle after the 776 BC Games. Olympiad 14-2 was the name of the second year after the thirteenth Olympics.

It may seem odd that the Greeks should base their dates around an athletics festival. In fact, as we have seen, the Olympics were much more than a religious and sporting occasion. They provided an opportunity for people from all over the Greek world to meet. Politicians made agreements, businessmen made deals, and people who had not seen each other for a long time met just to have a good time.

A bronze discus with the terms of the Olympic Truce written on it.

The Olympic Truce

Every four years the Greek states obeyed what is known as the Olympic Truce. The Truce was written on a bronze discus kept in the Temple of Hera. It said that all the states taking part in the Games were forbidden to:

- Go to war
- Carry on a dispute in the law courts
- Execute criminals

Truce Bearers from the state of Elis travelled to every Greek state taking part in the Games and announced the terms of the Truce. Originally, the Truce lasted for one month. Later, this was extended to three months to protect visitors travelling long distances to get to and from the Games. People who broke the Truce were heavily fined.

> 'The Olympic Truce is written on a discus. The writing is not in a straight line, but in a circle around the edge of the discus.'
>
> Pausanias, *Description of Greece*, c. AD 150.

ΥΦΧΨ
ΜΝΞΟΠΡΣΤΥΦΧΨΩ

The Greeks at war: the warrior Achilles slays his enemy Penthesileia. During the three-month Olympic Truce such bloodshed was forbidden.

Officials and judges

Elis tried to keep out of the wars and conflicts that so often divided other Greek city-states. This was important if the Games were to be respected and the Truce obeyed.

About ten *Hellanodikai* (this word means 'Judges of the Greeks' in ancient Greek) were chosen by lot from among the citizens of Elis. It was the job of the Hellanodikai to run the Games. They dressed in purple robes and were organizers as well as judges. The Hellanodikai were famous for their fairness.

Preparing for the Games was a massive task. It took almost a year. The site was weeded and cleaned up, because it had not been used since the previous Games. The Truce Bearers were sent out and accommodation was prepared for the athletes and visitors. At least a month before the festival opened, the first competitors started to arrive.

Training

Greek athletes took their training almost as seriously as modern sports men and women. They had to swear an oath saying that they had been training for ten months. The rules of the Games also said that they had to be in the city of Elis a month before the competitions began. Here, their training was supervised by the Hellanodikai. Most athletes had their own professional trainers as well.

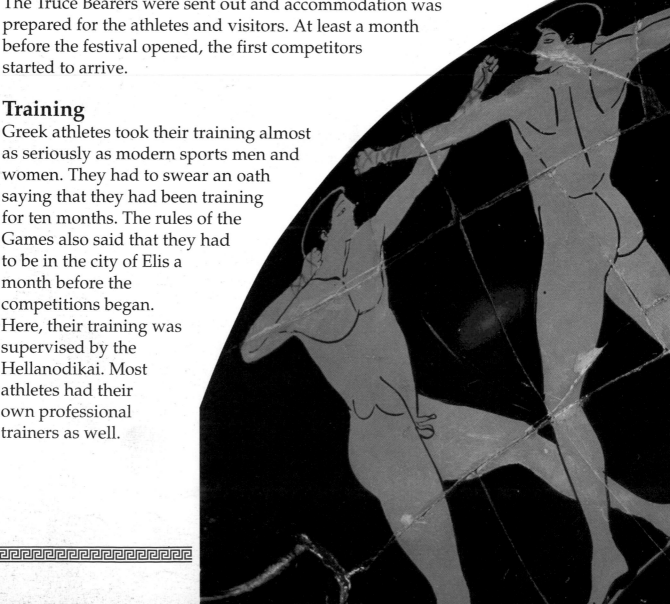

A trainer with a rod in his hand watches over boxing practice. The boxers' hands were wrapped in leather strips, called thongs, so punches were very painful.

The whole city was taken over by the Games. There were three gymnasiums in use in the town, and the market place was turned into a practice race track! The Hellanodikai controlled the athletes' diets and work programmes, and competitors who did not come up to scratch were disqualified before they even reached Olympia.

'You want to be an Olympic champion? Hang on a minute and think what's involved . . . You will have to do what you are told, follow a strict diet, stick to your training schedule in all weathers and follow your coach as you would a doctor.'

Epictetus, *Discourses*, c. AD 100.

ΡΣΤΥΦΧΨ

ΜΝΞΟΠΡΣΤΥΦΧΨΩ

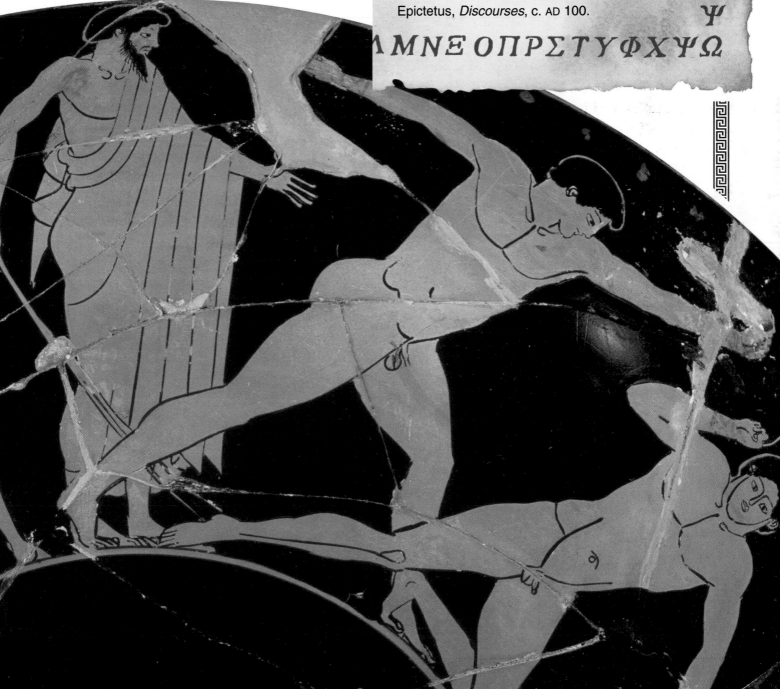

The Sacred Way

Two days before the Games began, the athletes, trainers, horses, chariots, Hellanodikai and other officials and guests set out for Olympia from the city of Elis. This 58-kilometre route was known as the Sacred Way, a reminder of the Games' religious beginnings. The Sacred Way travelled along the Greek coastline, which stretches further west today than it did during the first century BC.

> 'You can easily recognize an athlete who has eaten too much. He has thick eyebrows, his collar bones stick out, he gasps for breath and he has rolls of fat round his waist.'
>
> Philostratos, *On Athletics*, c. AD 210.

People travelled from Greek settlements as far apart as Spain and Egypt to attend the Games.

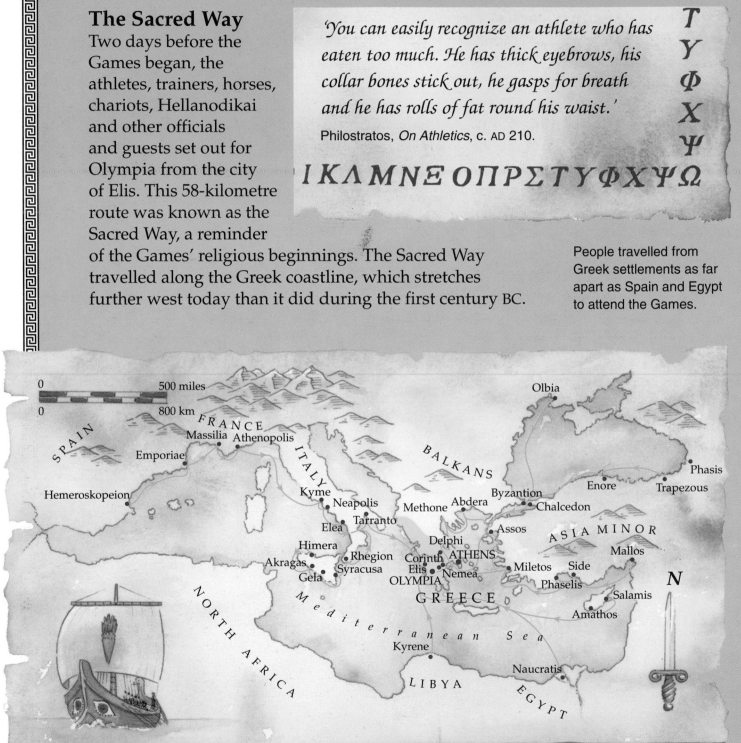

The brilliant procession took two days to complete, stopping at different points along the way for religious festivities. For example, at Piera, on the boundary of Olympia, a pig was sacrificed.

The spectators arrive

As the procession was making its way to Olympia, spectators began arriving from all over Greece and from Greek settlements across southern Europe and the fringes of Africa and Asia (see map opposite). Wealthy visitors sailed up the River Alpheios and others came by donkey or on foot. Merchants and food-sellers came along, too, eager to sell food and souvenirs to the crowds.

Top officials and important foreign visitors stayed at the *Leonidaion*. This was like a huge hotel just outside the south-west corner of the Altis. Other visitors had to make do as best they could with tents, blankets on the ground or wooden shelters. By the time the procession arrived at Olympia, the site was jam-packed.

The greatest festival in the Greek world was ready to begin.

Spectators crowd on to a stand to cheer on their favourites in the chariot race. This picture comes from a pot from 580BC.

5 Let the Games Begin!

The number and order of Olympic events continually changed over the centuries. During the first Games, only sprint races were held. Later, a great variety of other events were introduced. Some (such as boxing) remained part of the programme, while others (such as mule cart races) were soon abandoned.

Akontists throwing the javelin from horseback. The name of this sport comes from the word *akon*, meaning 'light wooden javelin'. This sport may once have been a part of the Games.

We do not really know what the original purpose of the Games was. It is possible that they were held to keep men fit for fighting. Events like throwing the javelin and the race-in-armour were certainly based on military skills. But other events were simply tests of athletic ability.

'The first people to exercise naked were the Spartans. They stripped off their clothes in public and rubbed themselves with oil after they had finished.'

Thucydides, *History of the Peloponnesian War*, fifth century BC.

ΑΒΓΔΕΖΗΘΙΚΛΜ

No clothes

When the Games began, athletes probably wore some kind of shorts. Later, athletes in most events competed naked.

No one is quite sure why this was. The Greeks themselves had two explanations. One was that a runner from Athens was about to win a race when his shorts fell down and tripped him up! The judges then made a rule that no one was to wear clothes, so that this could not happen again.

Another story tells us that, in 720 BC, a runner from Megara lost his shorts half-way through a long-distance race, but still went on to win. This set a new fashion for naked running, which was followed from then onwards.

It is more likely, however, that the Greeks competed naked because they were very proud of their bodies. They rubbed themselves with olive oil. This may have been to make themselves look more gleaming and muscular.

Young men playing a game with sticks and a ball.

Running

There were three lengths of running race at the ancient Olympic Games.

- The *stade* was a sprint of one length of the stadium. Runners began the race from a standing start, with their toes gripping grooves in a starting-line. The stade was the most famous Olympic race and the whole Olympiad was named after the winner of this race.
- The *diaulos* was also a sprint, but over two lengths of the stadium. The runners had to turn around the post at the far end and then return.
- The long-distance race was known as the *dolichos*. Competitors ran 20 or 24 lengths of the stadium. The dolichos was the first race in the programme of running events.

Occasionally, a brilliant athlete won all three running races. He was known as a *triastes*, or 'three-timer'. The greatest triastes of all was Leonidas of Rhodes, who was a three-timer in four Games in a row between 164 and 152 BC. The people of Rhodes were so proud of Leonidas that they worshipped him as a hero.

The original Olympic starting grid (main picture). The athletes gripped the grooves with their toes.

This vase painting from the fifth century BC shows runners in a long-distance race approaching the turning post at the end of the stadium.

Race-in-armour

The race-in-armour, or *hoplitodromos*, was the last race of the Games. Twenty-five runners wearing their helmets and greaves (leg armour worn over the shins) and carrying their shields, ran down the stadium to the shouts of the crowd. Sometimes, the athletes dropped their shields or collided with each other.

'Stade runners compete in separate heats and then run in the final. So the winner of the stade has in fact won two races.'

Pausanias, *Description of Greece*, c. AD 150.

ΠΡΣΤΥΦΧΨΩ

Pentathlon

Penta means five in Greek; pentathletes competed in five events. We are not sure how an athlete won. There was no points system, as we have in the pentathlon today. All we know is that, if an athlete won the first three events, he was declared the winner and the last two events were then cancelled. The five events were:

Running

The running competition is described on page 26.

Wrestling

The wrestling competition is described on pages 30-31.

Long jump

The long jump was a competition that was held only as a part of the pentathlon. In many ways, it was completely different from the modern long jump. The athletes carried weights in both hands, each weighing up to 4 kilograms. By swinging their arms, they used the weights to help them jump further. Rhythm and timing were essential, so music was

In the long jump, athletes jumped from a standing start instead of running up to the sandpit like modern jumpers.

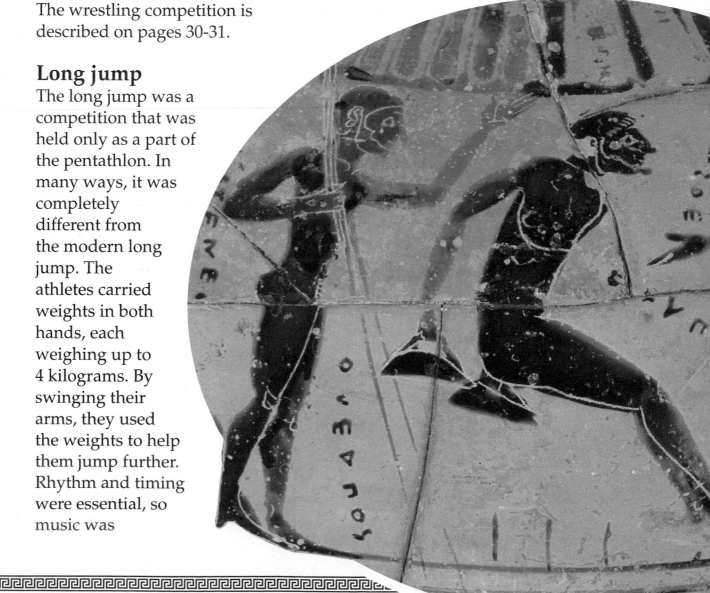

sometimes played as the athletes jumped. The best jumpers are said to have travelled over 16 metres (the best jumpers today travel about 8 metres without weights).

Discus

Greek discuses were made of bronze, lead or marble. As far as we can tell, the Greeks were not as expert as modern discus-throwers. They regarded a throw of 30 metres as being excellent. This would not win a school sports day today. This might be because the original Olympic discuses were very heavy. None have survived, but other ancient Greek discuses weigh over 6 kilograms. The heaviest modern discus weighs only 2 kilograms.

Javelin

Ancient Olympic javelin-throwing was quite like our modern-day sport. The main difference was in the javelin itself. Greek javelins were made of elder-wood, with a leather loop tied round the middle. The thrower held the javelin with the leather loop. The best throws travelled more than 100 metres. The modern-day record for men's javelin-throwing is 95.66 metres.

'Pentathletes have the most beautiful bodies, because they are built for speed and strength.'

Aristotle, *Rhetoric*, fourth century BC.

ΣΤΥΦΧΨ

ΠΡΣΤΥΦΧΨΩ

Long jumpers held these weights in their hands and swung them forward when they jumped to help them go further.

Boxing

Greek boxers were tough. The fighters wore strips of leather tied around their hands which did not do much to soften the blows. They did not fight in a ring but moved around over a wide area. All sorts of blows were allowed. One fighter is said to have jabbed his fingers into his opponent's stomach so hard that he pulled out his guts! A fight ended when one man surrendered, or passed out – or died.

A bronze sculpture of a Greek boxer. Look at his hands to see the Greek version of boxing gloves – strips of leather wound around the hands.

Wrestling

Greek wrestlers were vicious. Fighters were not allowed to bite or dig their fingers into soft parts of the body, such as the eyes or groin, but they were allowed to do anything else.

They could certainly yank opponents by the hair, which is why some wrestlers shaved their heads.

There were two types of wrestling match. In one, the aim was to throw an opponent to the ground three times. In the other, the wrestlers fought on until one of them surrendered. He did this by waving a finger in the air. All fighters covered their bodies in oil, to make it difficult for an opponent to get hold of them.

'When he saw the athletes biting and breaking the rules of the pankration, he said, "I'm not surprised fans call them 'lions' rather than athletes!".'

Lucian, *Demonax*, c. AD 150.

Pankration

The *pankration*, a combination of boxing and wrestling, was the roughest sport of all. Gouging, biting and kicking were thought to be signs of weakness. But they were still used by some fighters, who also punched, threw, strangled and twisted each other until one of them gave up.

Sostratos was famous for breaking his opponents' fingers during the pankration. The stocky 'Leaping Weight' specialized in wrenching ankles out of their sockets. Polydamas defeated all his opponents, including a lion that once attacked him!

A throw! The judge watches carefully as a pankration fighter hurls his opponent to the ground.

Horse races

There seem to have been three types of horse race at the original Olympics. One was a straightforward race over about 1,200 metres. The others were a race for colts (young male horses), and another for mares (female horses). In the mares' race the rider had to dismount and run beside his horse to the finishing line. We still have an event like this in modern horse competitions.

The big difference between Olympic horse racing and racing today is that the Greeks rode without saddles or stirrups. Neither had been invented. Jockeys needed greater skill to avoid falling off their horses.

A vase painting of the fifth century BC showing a horse race. This vase was awarded as a prize to the winner of the race.

Victory cro[wns]

The victors' cr[...]
from the sacre[...]
golden sickle. [...]
displayed on [...]
We are not sur[...]
crowns were b[...]
temple and the[...]

Speeches a[nd ...]

The ancient G[...]
Olympic victo[...]
special celebra[...]
banquet. There[...]
private parties[...]
night with win[...]
speeches, song[...]
and hymns to [...]

For the cha[...]
celebrations di[...]
when the Gam[...]
As soon as the [...]
home, there w[...]
more feasts an[...]
Everyone wan[...]
the new star w[...]
brought their [...]

Spectators watch a[...]
champion being cr[...]
with his victory wre[...]

Chariot races

Chariot races were a tremendous spectacle: teams of steaming horses thundering over the dusty track; grim-faced charioteers gripping the reins as they swayed and skidded around the bends; the roaring spectators; terrifying crashes; last-second overtaking. For many people in the crowd the chariot races were the most exciting part of the whole Olympics.

There were four different types of race: two- or four-horse chariots, pulled by either colts or older horses. The distance raced might be as much as 12 kilometres. The chariots were very light, made of wood and basketwork, and decorated with paint and precious metals. The charioteers were paid professionals. Very few horse owners drove their own team of horses – it was far too dangerous. Chariots were entered by individuals, groups and even by states. The prize went to the owner of the horses, not the charioteer.

'My father turned his attention to preparing race horses, something only the very rich can afford to do. He was so successful that he beat all his rivals and . . . won first, second and third places.'

Isokrates, *Team of Horses*, c. 380 BC.

A painting of horses and chariots from a Greek vase made between 900 and 720 BC.

Olympia disappears

The Temple of Zeus was destroyed by fire in AD 426. Over the next century, waves of barbarian invaders raided the Olympic site. Buildings were looted and then left to fall into ruin. Grass grew over the stadium and the hippodrome.

What man had begun, nature completed. Earthquakes rocked the site, toppling the temples and monuments. First the River Kladeos then the River Alpheios burst their banks, and whole buildings were swept away. Storms washed rocks and earth down from the Hill of Kronos. By the end of the Middle Ages (c. 1500) the site of the original Olympics was completely hidden beneath 4 metres of silt. Olympia had disappeared.

It took archaeologists many years of painstaking work to uncover the Olympic site so that we can visit it today. This is a passage leading from the Altis to the running track.

Rediscovery

Eighteenth-century Europeans were fascinated by the world of ancient Greece and Rome. A group of British scholars from the Dilettanti Society employed the young archaeologist Richard Chandler to travel to Greece and search for the site of the famous Olympic Games. In 1766 he struck lucky. Digging through the dirt at the foot of the Hill of Kronos, he began to uncover the remains of Olympia.

Other people followed up Chandler's discovery. In 1829 a team of French archaeologists explored the site more carefully. However, it was almost another fifty years before Olympia was properly investigated. A number of people were inspired by the idea of restarting the Games. They were supported by the new German emperor, Kaiser Wilhelm I. With permission from the Greeks, the German government paid for a full-scale archaeological dig lasting six years. Gradually, year by year, the glory of Olympia was brought to light.

Once many layers of earth had been removed, the Olympic stadium was revealed, seen here from the entrance.

A new Olympics?

The young French nobleman Pierre de Fredi, Baron de Coubertin, read the report of the German excavations at Olympia. He gave a speech to the Union of Athletic Sports in Paris, in which he suggested reviving the Olympic Games. Coubertin was worried by the level of fitness of people living in industrial towns and he was impressed by the part played by sport in some British schools and American colleges. He also wanted to find a way for nations to compete against each other without going to war.

'The last subject on the paper is . . . an international agreement that will revive the Olympic Games . . . so that every four years the world's athletes may come together . . . for honest and peaceful contests.'

Baron de Coubertin's speech, delivered in Paris in 1892.

Ζ Τ Υ Φ Χ Ψ

Θ Ι Κ Λ Μ Ν Ξ Ο Π Ρ Σ Τ Υ Φ Χ Ψ Ω

His suggestion of restarting the Games caught on. In 1894, the International Olympic Committee was set up and the first modern Olympic Games were arranged to be held in Athens in 1896.

On your marks! The start of the first modern Olympics in 1896.

The 1896 Olympics

Thirteen nations sent 311 competitors to compete in the 1896 Games. The athletic events were held in a new marble stadium, based on the one built in about 350 BC. It was only 333.3 metres long (modern tracks measure 400 metres), so the runners had to slow down on the tight bends! The USA sent the strongest team entry and won nine of the twelve track and field events. There were some unusual events too, such as bell-ringing, and a swimming race open only to sailors from the Greek Navy.

The discus was reintroduced – this was the first time a sportsman had thrown one since ancient times!

The most successful new event was the marathon race of about 26 miles (about 42 kilometres). It was based on the story of the Greek soldier, Pheidippides, who ran all the way to Athens from the battlefield of Marathon, where the Greeks won a great victory over the Persians in 490 BC. The new Games were a huge success. More were planned, to be held every four years, just as they had been in ancient times.

The marble stadium built in Athens specially for the 1896 Olympics.

Medals awarded at the 1896 Olympics (top and left).

Ancient and modern Games

The modern Olympics have survived to this day and, just as in ancient Greece, an Olympic victory is every athlete's highest goal.

The Games are still held every four years, as in ancient times. But there have been exceptions – three Games (1916, 1940 and 1944) were cancelled because of the two World Wars. The Olympics have become a focus of world attention, and governments or extreme political groups have used the Games to draw attention to their causes. In 1972, terrorists broke into the Olympic village at the Munich games, murdered two of the Israeli team and took nine hostages. A policeman, five terrorists and all of the hostages were killed after a failed rescue attempt.

Other Olympic meetings have been overshadowed by disputes between the USA and the former USSR. The USA refused to attend the Moscow Olympics in 1980 and the USSR refused to attend the Los Angeles Olympics in 1984.

'The important thing in the Olympic Games is not winning but taking part.'
Baron de Coubertin, 1896.

Π Ρ Σ Τ Υ Φ Χ Ψ
Τ Υ Φ Χ Ψ Ω

The final of the women's 10,000 metres race at the Barcelona Olympics in 1992.

The same but different

There are a number of important differences between the ancient and the modern Olympics. For example:

- Each modern Olympics is held in a different city. Recently these have been Seoul (South Korea) in 1988, Barcelona (Spain) in 1992 and Atlanta (USA) in 1996.
- There is now an Olympic flag. The five rings on the flag represent the five continents from which competitors come.
- Since 1908 there have been separate Olympics for winter and summer sports.
- Women have competed in the same Olympics as men since 1928.
- Modern Olympic stadiums hold almost 100,000 spectators, while the world-wide television audience is over 2.5 billion.
- The summer Games last for over a fortnight and involve over twenty types of event, from archery to yachting.
- The first three winners in each event are honoured with gold, silver and bronze medals.

People from every corner of the globe come together to compete in the modern Olympic Games. The Games remain one of the ancient Greeks' finest legacies to the modern world.

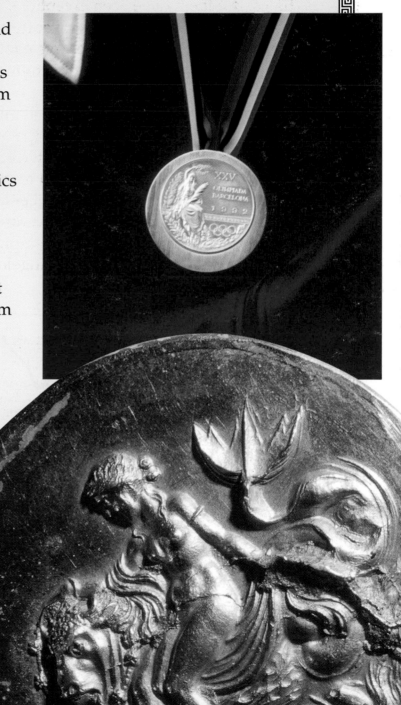

A modern Olympic gold medal from the 1992 Games in Barcelona.

A gold medal awarded at a Greek Games in the third century AD.

Glossary

Alexander the Great
(356-323 BC) Son of Philip of Macedon, Alexander came to his father's throne when only twenty. Macedon is in north-east Greece. Alexander's skill as a warrior and general became legendary.

Altis
The sacred olive grove at Olympia.

Ambassadors
High-ranking officials sent abroad to represent their states.

Archaeologists
People who find out about the past by digging up and examining ancient remains.

Asia Minor
The land between the Black Sea, the Mediterranean Sea and the Aegean Sea. This land is now a part of modern-day Turkey.

Banquet
A large special feast.

Barbarian
The ancient Greek name for peoples who did not speak Greek.

Citizen
A free-born Athenian whose parents were Athenian.

City-states
Greek cities that governed themselves, had their own laws, customs, weights, measures and, sometimes, their own ways of measuring time.

Civil war
A war between different groups within one city or country.

Eloquent
To speak or write well.

Hellanodikai
The ten judges who organized and guided the Games.

Heraia
The Games for women only. The Heraia was organized by sixteen important female citizens of the city of Elis.

Hippodrome
The horse-racing arena.

Inscription
Another name for writing.

Neutral
Avoiding taking sides in a war.

Olympia
The original Olympic site.

Olympiad
The four-year period between Olympic Games.

Oracle
A temple or shrine where Greeks could consult the gods about their future. People could ask the gods a question and priests would translate noises, such as rustling leaves, as the words of the gods.

Palaistra
A building for bathing and preparing for competition. Fighting and jumping competitions took place in the palaistra.

Pankration
The name of the most violent of the ancient Greek fighting competitions.

Peloponnese
The southern part of Greece. The main cities of the Peloponnese during ancient Greek times were Sparta and Corinth.

Pentathlon
A sports competition of five events.

Sacred
A religious object, place, person.

Sacred Way
The route of the 58-kilometre journey from the city of Elis to Olympia.

Sacrifice
To kill a person or an animal to please a god. Sacrifices were often carried out by priests and priestesses.

Sceptre
A staff held by an important person or god.

Scholars
People who are experts in one or more areas of knowledge.

Settlements
The name given to the communities groups of people live in.

Seven Wonders of the Ancient World
The seven buildings and objects considered to be people's greatest achievements. They were: the Pyramids of Egypt; the Hanging Gardens of Babylon; Pheidias' statue of Zeus at Olympia; the Colossus of Rhodes; the Temple of Artemis at Ephesus; the Mausoleum of Halicarnassus; and the Lighthouse of Alexandria.

Sickle
A knife with a curved blade and a short handle used in farming.

Silt
Layers of mud, clay and tiny stones carried by water onto the land.

Sparta
One of the most important Greek city-states on the Peloponnese.

Truce
An agreement not to fight.

Twelve Labours of Heracles
Heracles was ordered to perform twelve tasks by King Eurystheus of Argos as punishment for killing his own children in a fit of madness. Most of these tasks were dangerous and thought to be impossible – so they required cunning and strength.

Time Line

Further Information

Books to read

Clare, J.D., *I Was There: Ancient Greece* (Riverswift, 1994)

Ganeri, Anita, *Eyewitness Guides: Ancient Greece* (Dorling Kindersley, 1993)

Jones, John Ellis, *History as Evidence: Ancient Greece* (Kingfisher, 1992)

Loverance and Wood, *See Through History: Ancient Greece* (Hamlyn, 1992)

Malan, J., *Indiana Jones Explores Ancient Greece* (Evans Brothers, 1993)

Williams, Susan A., *Look Into The Past: The Greeks* (Wayland, 1993)

Wright, R., *Craft Topics: Greeks* (Franklin Watts, 1994)

Books for older readers

Finley, M.I and Pleket, H.W., *The Olympic Games: The First Thousand Years* (Chatto & Windus, 1976)

Harris, H.A., *Greek Athletes and Athletics* (Hutchinson, 1964)

Harris, H.A., *Sport in Greece and Rome* (Thames and Hudson, 1972)

Raschke, Wendy J., *The Archaeology of the Olympics* (University of Wisconsin Press, 1988)

Swaddling, Judith, *The Ancient Olympic Games* (British Museum Publications, 1980)

Sweet, Waldo E., *Sport and Recreation in Ancient Greece* (Oxford University Press, 1987)

Places to visit

If you are ever fortunate enough to spend a holiday in Greece or go there on a school trip, you may be able to visit Olympia, the site of the original Olympics. If you fly by the Greek airline, notice its name – OLYMPIC!

Index

Numbers in **bold** indicate an illustration. Words in **bold** can be found in the glossary on page 46.